Romanticized Ruin

Erica Adelaide Johnson

Published by: Erica Adelaide Johnson

Illustrations by: Erica Adelaide Johnson

Cover Design by: Erica Adelaide Johnson

ISBN-13: 978-1-7355967-2-3

For those that made it through and wonder what next. Allowing yourself to look towards the future doesn't mean you lose sight of where you've been. It simply means it is time to turn the page. Your story so far is still yours to tell. The book just isn't finished yet.

Table of Contents

Section I:
Restless Relics

Section II:

Threats of Thievery

Section III:

Sacred Sorrows

Section IV:

Mausoleum of Memories

Introduction

No one warns you how daunting it is to create a life in the stillness beyond tragedy and trauma. It is a tricky notion to truly live when you've only known yourself as a survivor for so long. Romanticized Ruin is for those who find themselves in the thick of that struggle.

This collection is about recognizing that there is so much more to your story and trusting that there is a way to move on while still honoring the events that shaped the strong, resilient person you have become. There are many facets to grief that linger long after the initial loss. Grief has a way of making us feel isolated when in reality it is one of the uniting foundations of humanity.

A life lived to the fullest is one that recognizes the beauty in experiencing the full spectrum of emotion that we all face eventually. We know joy because there has been sadness. We know confidence because there has been doubt. We know love because there has been loss. That is what it is to be human.

Section I:
Restless Relics

SOME PRICELESS RELIC

I have held my hurt
like some priceless relic.
I have erected
this museum to hold it
locked behind glass
for safe keeping
like some thief might come
and steal away my experiences.

Romanticized Ruin

Perhaps I have done so
because much of what remains
of my memory of my own life
has been taken from me,
locked away behind impenetrable walls
for the sake of my own sanity.
It was not a choice, but a necessity
lest this fragile structure
I have spent my entire life fortifying
come crashing down.

TIRED

I whisper, "I'm tired,"
to the walls that won't respond.
This has become my refrain
on the lonely morning drives
to the place where my soul seeps
slow from the vein.

Here I feel nothing
but the surrender of the keys
beneath my fingertips
that offer naught
at the end of the day
except maybe a place to stay
in this long monotonous log
of the business that must be done
    by someone,
        by anyone,
           but for now,
           by this miserable one.

They don't see how this weariness
is not the kind eased
by some blissful sleep.
No, this fatigue adds density to the frame
as if I am sinking in the mud
but somehow, also hollow enough
to fade in the breeze.
And I can't help but wonder
how much easier it might be
if I did go
where the winds wished to take me,
someplace where I could appreciate
the glow of days as they bleed into the next
without my heart bruising itself
in some frantic effort to escape its cage.

OTHER SIDE

Why is it so easy to

romanticize the harsh years,
but the pleasant moments now
seem scattered like dust?
All the things I hoped for
in the dark times
burst like tiny stars and die out
before my tired eyes.
I scarcely have the time to admire them.
So, I bow my knee in reverence
once more
to the only pieces of me
that seem capable of sustaining.

I think I may have

buried my own potential

in the plot that survival left me.

It seems a strange degree of cruel

to have made it through to the other side

and somehow still be compelled

to seek yet another side.

Will the glimmer of what I find

around the next corner

ever fill the void left in me?

I am weary and restless

for the person I feel is lost to me

somewhere between

what I should have been

and who I have become.

WASTE

All I see is waste in the spaces
that fail to find any excuse
to be called great.
They are the tears
that brim and spill
silent like the lies
I use to hide.
They are the heartbeats
that falter and breed
breathless panic
beneath clear skies.
How long will it be
enough to survive?
How long will it feel
like all I do is survive?

Erica Adelaide Johnson

CURRENTS OF DESPAIR

The disappointment came in waves.
I was caught in the current of despair
fueled by the multitude of ways
I had failed to be remarkable.
the frigid waters chilled by
the inability of my own endeavors
to satisfy a purpose.
I have always struggled to make sense of it.
The only sweetness lies in anticipation.
No treat is meant to endure.
The tender knowing of what shall pass
from what is to what was
leaves a palpable bitterness.
a flavor that has tinged
every moment and memory without end.

PERMANENCE

How long have I ached
to see you take interest?
There was a longing
planted in me long ago
for you to want to know me,
deep enough that I lost sight
of what I should want
to know about myself.
This road is dust,
no permanence yet forged.

I seek to travel it

slowly to savor

all the bits and pieces

of my being I left by the wayside

for the shiny allure

of some grandeur

I thought might await me

down the bustling highways

we are told lead

to what we should want.

I abandon that course now

for the possibility

that my true desires

are not those given to me

but instead, are buried within.

I must excavate my own expectations
to know what hopes
must be placed at the forefront
if even I dare to dream
of contentment or
perhaps one day,
the radical idea of happiness.

HOLLOW

I know that I once knew you,
but a stranger seems too familiar
a name to call you now.
The person I am is not the person
who knew you.
In that way, I think perhaps
we both mourn,
for the days have given way
to whatever pressures have
worn away at the shiny youthful notions
once cemented in our bones.
Hollow are the spaces
that my dreams once filled.

The weight of these aspirations
cling to me like shackles.
I avoid the deep waters now
for I know just how easily
these weights would drag me
down to the watery grave
where perhaps the noise
might finally be
hushed by the deep,
as it seems the only place
vast enough to hold this emptiness.

SILENT

This pain lands silent on your ears.

You inflict this hurt

like only the innocent can,

as they are blind to true suffering.

But how can't you see?

Weren't you right there beside me

through those same desolate days,

or did you merely fill the space?

This hurt is rawer for your proximity to it,

and still, your inability

to understand its toll

has a way of eating at me.

Romanticized Ruin

How could I be someone dear to you
when you have closed your heart
to what has shattered mine?

All I have ever needed from you
or anyone really,
is to be seen,
but even you deny that to me.
What a draining notion is it
to be invisible.

It's true, I wanted nothing more
than to hide from the world,
but I never wanted to hide from you.
Yet, it seems you may force me to.

PLAGUED BY THE KNOWING

Hours of typing
but not the story I wish to tell.
Straining eyes in the stark light,
I am plagued by the knowing
that each tick marking the passing minute
adds only to the missing
pieces lost to wasted time.
But they would never let you
think such a thing of the toil
they place on you,
the willing laborer in search of something
worth laboring for.

THE JAR

I am the jar
with the misprinted expiration date.
Hold me up to the light.
Turn me over and over
in your hands,
fervently seeking out the truth hidden
in plain sight misconstrued.
My life has been the conveyor belt.
Round and round I go
stuck in place at the end of the line
that never seems to switch off.

I am suspended but never static.

Your gaze passes over me

ever settling on the option

that does not hide itself from you.

I was forged as a trick

that will leave me unused

in the worst of ways.

What I might offer

is left to spoil

as they push me to the back yet again.

SUFFOCATED

We are raised voices
and shoulders turned
blind in the dark of night.
We are beds shared
but oceans apart.
I am cursed by this need
to share with you because
there is no one else,
and regret floods me
every time.

But like the coastal residents,
I rebuild faithfully after every storm
in the futile effort of hope
that some other fate lies in store.
You burn me in ways
that are not the ones
I yearned for.
Your gaze is seething.
I am suffocated by both
your presence and your absence.
How our existence is a curse
and a blessing to each other.
Only time will allow
one force to conquer the other.

ALTER OF ACHIEVEMENT

My reflection pleads with me
to hold fast to the ambitions
aimed square at my heart in reverence
of the many days of my youth
spilt before the alter of achievement.
How I sacrificed before it
the lifeblood of every intrigue
until I was bled dry,
the husk of who remained
weighed down by expectation alone,
no happiness heavy enough
to keep me in place.
It was fear that fueled me
and kept me at bay
day after day.

SICKNESS

Why must it be a sickness
to offer thoughts that do not align?
Who is the judge of which of these
is an ailment
and which is the cure?
I tell myself a hundred times
to keep my lips pressed in a stern line.
Stop pouring out the thoughts
that no one wishes to hear.
The fortunate among us
let these darker things lie
in the depths of their minds.

They do not seek them out,
and they do not appreciate
when you do so for them.
They say that dwelling on such things
must not be healthy,
but I dare say
letting them strangle me in silence
seems far worse a fate.
I thrust them into the daylight
so that at least when
they get the best of me,
my undoing is not some mystery.
The crime will not go unsolved
even if the criminal roams free.

SUPPOSITION

How many times has my purpose
been asked of me?
Still yet, how many times
have I myself been inclined
to be my own haunting presence?
In the shadows, I pose
the sneering question on my lips.

What a disease purpose can become
when we confuse worth
with expectation.

Romanticized Ruin

How slow we were to learn that
nothing ever meets supposition on par.
We find that for better or worse
both results will cast clouds over our view
of what is to come.
We are destined to miscalculate
and marvel at our own naive view
of what we thought awaited us.

Erica Adelaide Johnson

HOSTAGE

You are not alone,
but you are lonely.
The ornate vase cracked ages ago
was left to weather these years
in a glass cage.
They would have you believe
such measures were for safe keeping,
but you are as much a hostage
to your own mind
as you are to the bitter care
you can't seem to loosen your hold on.

You've always held on a bit too tight,
and in time, all things
you have desperately gripped
have found a way
to loosen themselves from you.
As much as you tried
to weave them into your story,
they ran from you
in search of something far more epic
than you could ever offer.
Who are you to blame them
for wanting more than you could give?
Isn't that all your days are filled with?

THE FOOL

What should I scrawl on this page
to be burned
after these endless days find
some way to give themselves over
to the after,
when I finally have the courage
to purge the ugly truth of the lies
I have told
over and over
to the fool
living in these bones?

STORM CHASER

I find myself at the mercy
of the sea seething
within me.

The storms that loom over these shores
are relentless,
lasting for days on end.

Somehow, I still seek them out.
I am the storm chaser
doomed by my own obsession.

I only ever wanted
to watch my own destruction.
How lucky I am to see this ruin firsthand.

It is so preciously personal

here in the wreckage.

I finally see all the parts of me scattered.

Perhaps as they were intended to be.

BURDENS

I awake to starlight
strangled by my own fear,
a gripping in my mind
reminding me of a thousand
things I cannot change,
and lording the cruelty of
my own misunderstanding
over me.

The sun's rise seems fictional,
some far-off escape
from the tragedy
that has forced its way
back through my door.

Might the hours beyond this endless night
free me from the burdens
that the dark so often brings me?

THE ABYSS

There are lives that I ache for
buried deep inside,
under mountains of rubble,
made from all the dreams
I was told to have.
I made these things mine
and forfeited all my time,
until one day the earth split open.
I stood at the edge of the chasm
suddenly called forth
to meet my destiny,
the one I had so cruelly left to ruin.
How will the dark of the unknown
embrace me?

I allow my weight to tip
over the edge into the abyss,
and if this is lost,
I may never wish to be found.
For what is there to know
when you have never known yourself?

ELUSIVE AS HAPPINESS

There are nights that my mind races
like a trail runner
through the thick undergrowth.
I almost crave the root that trips me,
for the quicker blood is drawn the sooner
I might wake from this tireless pursuit.
See I was mistaken
in those small, hopeful years.
I was never destined to pursue,
much less pursue a thing
as elusive as happiness.
No, I know now,
I was only ever destined to be pursued.
I always hated running, but I learned
to be just quick enough to escape.

It has always been about survival,
in some shape or form.
I used to run from judgment
and the shame of falling short.
These days I think maybe
not much has changed,
except the judgment I run from now
is fueled only by my anxieties
and the darker things
I haven't been brave enough to name.
The shadows that surround me now
are my own.

CRUEL INTERPRETATIONS

This restless mind
is doomed to race.
If only it were the worthy thoughts
destined to win.
My edges are bare,
and I am left raw in the room,
exposed to the cruel interpretation
my mind portrays to me.
I am endlessly searching
for some reason
in all of the monotony,
but it seems I am cursed
in more ways than most.

See I know that I am wasting

this precious time,

and it is a futile endeavor

to savor or surrender it.

The toil is told again and again

like the words spoken themselves

might offer meaning to the meaningless.

IMPENETRABLE

I press my fingertips
against the glass once more
just to give myself reason
to wipe the marks away.
No one roams these halls but me.
What was once the thrill
of holding the only key
to this particular sanctuary
has grown to be a curse
in more ways than one.
My solitude used to offer comfort,
but now I think perhaps
I was crafting my own prison
without even realizing it.

I should give myself credit,

this fortress is in fact impenetrable.

I am safe, but so is the world outside

from whatever I might have

once contributed.

The silence is filled with the echoes

of my own doubts spiraling.

What good could I possibly have had

to offer anyhow?

This is the thought that has served

as the foundation of every wall

I have ever erected.

All I have ever been is a ghost of misfortune.

TROPHIES

There is a certain reliance
at the center of my familiarity
with these relics and their preciousness.
For what are these pieces
in my collection but ordinary objects
elevated to the status of trophies
purely for their proximity to the tragedies.
Their importance lies
only in what they have seen,
and I think perhaps,
it is the same for me.
I fear there may be nothing deeper
once the final ashes are cleansed.

My story has always been my survival,

but such a tale grows tired.

I have to consider now

that nothing lies ahead

that could ever give meaning

beyond what lies in the past.

Am I destined to join these relics

behind the glass?

Might my only contribution

be what has already came to pass?

UNENDING DREAM

I know that I am a stranger now
when you see me,
but what you do not realize,
is that it was the stranger
you knew all those years.
This shadow is all I have ever been,
try as I might to imitate the sunlight.
The warmth I have fought to absorb
flees from me the moment
the sun fades from the sky.
All of life's simple fruits have alluded me,
like I am in some unending dream
where I am cursed to always move
just a bit too slow to keep them
in my grasp.

Erica Adelaide Johnson

I pinned up these feelings,
painted canvas with blood and tears,
like making art of my pain
could offer perspective.
But these relics have grown restless,
born from a mind that has never felt
like there was a place for it to find refuge.
Decades of running now and trying
desperately to drown it out,
from the very moment of recollection
to the tired second passing even now.

COWARD

What if I wasn't joking
when I said my insides
were cracked
like plastic grown brittle
in the harsh heat?
What should have brought
warmth and light
left only dust to be
scattered in the night.
See I am held together
with the glue made only
of what I won't dare allow through.
I couldn't tell you
the thoughts that build inside.
You would only run and hide.

I don't know that I could ever
consider myself a coward,
if only because it is frightening
to be left with this cruel monster
who lives in the reflection
and the corners of my mind.
For all of my shortcomings,
I must consider the small part of me
brave for standing in opposition
when she knows the odds
are never in her favor and the stakes
just keep stretching higher.
The ground is so far away,
but somehow what lies below
has never felt more threatening.

Section II:
Threats of Thievery

Erica Adelaide Johnson

THEY WERE MINE

Why is it that memory has a sinister
way of sneaking up on you in the hours
where dreams bleed into reality?
I don't often let myself remember,
but the flashes become the flood.
In an instant, I am reminded
of what was
and what seems to my waking mind
that it never could have been.
A torrent of every beautiful
and horrific memory
is laid out before me.
My own mind seems to prod at me.
What would I give to go back?

Would I dare live such things again
if I could, even though I barely
survived them the first time?
Yes, a sure resounding answer.
For all the hurt and anger,
they were mine.
These experiences are warm and comforting
like the home lost to time.
But they also hold
those same cold, empty halls
I wandered when that home
became a strange place
filled only with echoes
of cries and laughter alike.

PRESERVED PAIN

Call this marble hall
the resting place of misery,
a perfectly preserved pain
on display lest you forget your way
back to the things that made you this way.

The steps here fall heavy
carrying the weight of all these woes.
Visitors say the curator must be so busy
holding up the ceiling
of this dilapidated structure.

They don't know how the keeper
cannot bear to watch this creation,
carved from bone and fed with blood,
collapse to cover the artifacts
that hold the history that forged the falling.

HIDDEN IMPRINT

Were you the stepping stone
removed from the garden late at night?
Dew fell on yellowed roots
exposed in its absence.
In time, life will flood
back in brilliant green,
and your steps will fall on moist earth
rather than rough concrete.
But your mind will cause you
to step where they once laid
as if they left some sort
of hidden imprint
revealed only in memory.

ABSENCE

A brass button lies abandoned,
forgotten on the stairs.
It makes no difference
if it was left behind
in leisure or lost in the rush.
When its owner reaches down in time
they will find its absence
a reminder of all that seems almost
destined to be left behind.
We never wish to leave
what we have come to know
at least not consciously.

But along the line

we recognize more and more

the absence of the little things

that seem so big now

that the weight of them

doesn't rest in our possession.

How easy it is to cherish something

once we know it

to be lost.

ALWAYS YOU

I call you,
emotions rolling in waves
that crash upon
cliffs of misguided memory.

I stroll with you
down paths paved
in the pale blue glow
of moments passed too soon.

I reach to you
in the absence of all else
to touch the one solid
notion of myself I have left.

I plead with you
to hold what we have built,
tender and tight,
through the most bitter of nights.

MILESTONES

Frost forms like a protective layer
shielding my heart
from the burning intensity
of you and all your
empty, golden promises.

This space has stretched
far beyond what I could have
fathomed in the time
that I considered you
my most treasured ally.

The milestones still ache,
but I feel relieved in their wake
because another day has passed
without your presence
shattering this carefully crafted glass.

REASON

Today the winds came
warm and out of place.
Powerful and possessive,
they reached for me,
and my heart did shift with them
eager as always
to be present and purposeful.

The trees did bend,
and my own arms did extend
as though we each
might embrace the sky.

I could not control
the smile I felt,
though I knew all the while
that it could not last.
The cold would creep in,
and somehow, I would still
find reason to be glad.

RECEIVER OF WOES

It never fails to perplex me
how I seem to have an allure
that calls people to speak their
woes to me.
I am the hearer of secrets
others wish to hide from the light.
For all the problems I have heard
and all the advice I have given,
I never seem able to help myself.
Then, as always, they vanish from me
when the need passes.

Another of my curses
manifested in my need
to be worth some sort of purpose.
The conversations come to me
but never out of companionship.
I am the receiver
when others fear being alone.
I have found
I'm not much for switching places.
I guess I just got used to
the safety of solitude.

MOMENTS

How strange is the moment that lingers,
sweet in the way that it clings to us,
and we, desperate in our efforts
to savor it, seem destined to squander it.
Fragile are the fleeting minutes
when we find ourselves suspended
in the bitter knowing
that this joy will fade
to be emulated
but never replicated.

So, I plead with you darling,
as I plead with myself,
learn to hold tight
with a tender grasp
that recognizes the rarity
of each moment that causes
the very compounds of your being
to sing in the same tune
as the life that surrounds you.

LONELY TOGETHER

The curse of humanity
seems to be resolute loneliness.
We are all lonely together,
and yet we never seem
to find companionship
in such shared strife.
Crowded rooms do not offer refuge.
People find ways to be alone anywhere.
We seek it out
as the burden of explanation
weighs heavier by the day.
But who am I to say?

Erica Adelaide Johnson

SCARRED

It makes no difference
if it was war or plague.
The land is scarred just the same.
Neighbors gather together
clutching tight to what remains,
the life before alien to them.
The faces of those around
are marked with the strain,
yet somehow, not really changed.

WHOLLY

I always hoped I would be someone
who had things to say
at the start and end of each day.
My experiences from the smallest of moments
to the life altering cataclysms
would shape my rhetoric
into some insightful story worth repeating.
I think I doubt that ability now.
I have become too numb
to cut the pain from my palms.
It seems all for naught, and
I the squanderer of the experiences
gifted me for the sake of perspective.

Erica Adelaide Johnson

My eyes close to all of it
as the exhaustion pours in,
like concrete it fills the cracks
until I am whole but wholly spent.
There is nothing left of who I was,
and with that person
so too have the aspirations
reduced to ruin.
It is that ruin that I hoped to hold,
preserved, if imperfect,
a reminder of all
that I was once capable of.

MEASUREMENTS

Might I ask you to measure
the worth of one's own misery?
It does pain me to wonder
how your own treasured aches
might align with those that have
seared their place beneath my skin
like stains set in ink
that shall stand to mark me marred
but never motionless
as I sway with the sea that surges within.

And how could those things,
even the ones secluded
in cages forged of bone
hidden far from sight,
ever stand to hold less weight
than the shackles we all proudly display?
We carry on,
the clanging of our own captivity
adding to the symphony of solemn sorrow.

DUST

The awakening to my undoing
was a sudden sorrow.
I forgot myself in the dust,
and the dreamer I was died there
before I even knew she was waning.
Now, it is as if my breaths come
easy on some days and struggle
through the sodden sorrow on others.
The worst of it is this,
that I am no closer to knowing
what I hope for,
if it ever be something more concrete
than mere survival.
I sometimes doubt I will make it,
but what even am I trying to make it to?

Erica Adelaide Johnson

CUP OF MEMORIES

The memories have dried up in me.
Some mornings I brew the tea just to see
a glimpse of who might have been,
the water boiled and poured ever slowly
to grant a steaming vision
of what I know must have been
even if only in some forgotten land.
The words run dry too sometimes,
but even their stubbornness
is no match for a cup of memories
cradled tenderly in my mind
pooling in the parts of my heart
where the age-old aches always seem to settle.
Might we gather
to read the tea leaves together?

DIRE

Call it what you may.
I cannot stay away.
The dire degree of it
only draws me nearer.
There is a sadness
that sits in the center
of my bones.
There are those that seek
to separate me from it,
replace it with something
a bit easier for discussion.

Erica Adelaide Johnson

I confess, I am fearful
that in its absence
all that I am might collapse.
I have lived so long
with its ever-present weight.
I doubt this structure
without its core.
Now, as I let that familiar presence
wash over me,
I wonder if there aren't
far worse things
to be filled with.

TO MAKE SOME PEACE

These aches run deeper still,
and I have long since abandoned
the search for their source.
I take them now only as necessity,
evidence of my existence
that is sometimes the only thing strong
enough to cut through the numbness.
I think it has stopped being sad,
and instead, this lingering sting
is in many ways my only companion.
After all, we cannot leave behind the horrors
that inhabit our minds.

We might as well try

to make some peace with them.

On the days that this peace is tired,

I am reminded of the chaos that brews

in the silence I fill with distractions.

Of all the things that fill me,

I think the fear of what

I may never bring to fruition

is what threatens to spill over the brim.

So, I will gladly embrace the discomfort

if only I can hand over this discouragement.

BRAVE

How peculiar a notion it is
to be considered brave,
for it relies so heavily on
one's measurement of circumstance
both outward and especially inward.
There are days that to be brave
is nothing more than taking a breath
when such an action seems impossible.
For what is it to be brave
if not to persist against every force
that tells you not to?

When the waves
of what would only be regret
flood over me,
I remember,
I don't want to die
before I've even found
the courage to live.
Even in the darkest pits,
I know there is so much life
beyond the struggle of survival.
I believe we all deserve a taste
of that plenty
before we are faced with the end.

TESTAMENT

The fogs cascades down
to surround in its ethereal shroud
the harrowing horrors
I have opened the door to once more.
For in the likelihood that all will vanish
in the rising sun that cuts
like daggers into the eyes
that are still sore from one too many
bitter tears cried,
there holds the consideration
that this weight will never truly lift.

To brave those forces,

　　　those voices,

　　　　　and leave them

hushed by the sheer will of refusal,

when all that is easy

is the hardest thing to ignore,

that is truly a feat worth facing.

BEYOND

It would be a lie to say
that there are not days
when the idea of carrying on
seems far more painful
than abandoning all of this
to the inevitability that
what could have been
may not have been what
should have been,
and what has been,
is all that perhaps
was meant to be.

And if this weight persists
at what point will I find no choice
but to surrender to it?
Those years I once envisioned
as a testament to my strength
now show me only the spaces
in which my own weaknesses
have become glaring sources of shame.
Surely, they can all see me
for the failure I have allowed
to seep into every great endeavor
I once felt compelled to pursue.

WHY DO I STILL LINGER?

There are lakes frozen over
in the midpoint of my heart,
and my mind is sore
from the thoughts forced
to swim beneath the ice.
This winter has lasted
longer than those that I used
to tell stories of.
But at some point, the season
grows tired, and it is so easy
to assume the tundra was
and is all that will ever be known.

So, why do I still linger
over the imagined soft crackle
of flames mere inches from my hand?
If I have truly given up,
where is the peace to be made
with this frigid, barren land?

DAYS LIKE THIS

My words run circles in my mind,
soundless and screaming
somehow at the same time.
I press a hand hard to my collarbone
like I might finally find a way
to ground myself,
but all I feel is the excruciating,
overwhelming electric hum
that never leaves a moment for rest.
I take a deep breath because
that is all to be done on days like this
as my mind runs itself off the rails
showing me a thousand ways I have failed
and another dozen ways in which
those failures will catch up with me.

Erica Adelaide Johnson

I am paralyzed by my own inadequacy
in every aspect, and still
I pour every ounce of me that I have left
into playing the part
I succumbed myself to.
These days I speak as little as I can
and try to hide the tremor in my hand.
I know one slip is all that stands
in the way of what I am breaking through
the person I try to be.

THE FEAR THAT COMPELS

For as long as I've been fighting
I've never found much skill in it.
My tactics have always been desperate,
and I am no stranger
to crawling my way through the dark.
Such circumstances
are inconducive to friendships,
and so, I have watched them fade
like my memories buried deep
in who I would have been.
Should I feel guilt that I mourn one more?

Erica Adelaide Johnson

This life is held here

in a golden box I scarcely open

for fear the light of it too will escape me.

So. I guard it

but never truly possess it.

There are those that would call me mad

to squander it,

but that is precisely

the fear that compels me

to leave it sealed away.

How is it that I hold

such a precious possession

in my own hands and still find

it stolen from me?

THE ONES WHO STAND WATCH

Tighten your grip on the roses
even as they wilt in your hand.
Feel time claim them
like the bones in the ground
for which you offer them.
Consider the words that died on your lips
and since lost their chance
to land on the ears of the living.

How fear grips us
as we fail even now
to capture the gifts of this life.
The heart does break for the ones
who stand watch over their years
instead of living them.

Erica Adelaide Johnson

VERSIONS OF MYSELF

We are all guilty
of romanticizing our own ruin,
as if the scars hidden beneath skin
and carved into bone
are all that was ever intended for us.

What might we be
without the tight grasp
on our own suffering?
Oh, forbid if its sting
might be allowed to fade.

Romanticized Ruin

What am I without
    where I have been,
        what I have seen?
Are these versions of myself
ever to be fully at rest?

Could there be something
buried even deeper?
I must consider if I loosened my grip
and it all slipped away,
could I still feel it
as if it were yesterday?
Am I doomed to be haunted
by who I could have been
for the rest of these days?

You must understand
the marks left by this life
both seen and unseen
cannot be erased so easily.

I do not have to cling to this weight
to keep myself grounded.

Section III:
Sacred Sorrows

SACRED SORROWS

Specters crowd my sight.
This place that once held
the dearest dreams of mine
now holds only those
dreams that have died.
This tomb has grown crowded,
much the same as my tired mind.
When there is such little space
for the possibility of what is to come
it is so easy to reason with oneself
that all that will ever be worth remembering
has already come and gone.

It was comforting to know
the things that had haunted me so
would never truly leave me.
And while I never wished to forget them,
there was danger that lay hidden in
the way I fashioned each pedestal
for the hurts that marred me.
In a way, healing became a harrowing idea.
What would be left if I were to allow
these sacred sorrows to be scattered
from my collection?
What a waste to have them
sold off piece by piece to the highest bidder.
What could I hope to ever find
to fill their place?

Soon it became a spectacle,

the idea of adding some foreign

hope to my reverent hall.

What I was seemed set in stone

just as I had allowed what had transpired

to be bonded to my bones.

It felt like the marble

had been placed carefully so long ago.

How could I ever allow

a disturbance of what was sealed away?

The awareness that I was suffocating

in this solitary place registered only briefly

for I myself had been fading away

since the beginning.

TARNISHED

In the days that came after,
I clung to my sorrows
like some sacred safety line,
that last thin thread that
could led me back to what I knew.
Some part of me must have known that it
was an ill-fated notion, but
still, I could not loosen my grip.
I had lost so much,
it felt that this could not be
one more thing I parted with.
So, I held them in the dark
and snuck glances as they slept.
All the while I was moving forward,
crafting new art,

placing my heart on a blank canvas, but
the influence of these indulgences
bled into every new thing.
The freedom sought in the unfamiliar was
tarnished by the same aches and miseries.
I could not see then
that I was forfeiting this fresh start.
I was squandering my new muse
for fear of the pieces
I had yet to fashion from the old.
I have learned since that a tragedy long-lived
grows tired and seeks for itself to live on
at the expense of the energy
only found in the hope for the future.

THE MUSEUM KEEPER

A long corridor stretches before me
leading to the glass globe
erected to hold this reverent reminder
of my own heart of stone.
What was once so full of red
now darkened
to hide itself among the shadows.

I am the museum's keeper,
protector of what is left.
The robbers shake the chains
that clothe the gates.
I keep my sword braced to defend
against the masses of unknown threats.

For when such art was worth nothing

you still were sore at the sight

of anyone's attention

not spared for your own.

WILD PLACES

What of the wild places?
Am I to call such beauty
a fleeting friend in passing
when my very making
aches to sink my sorrows
in the lands that offer themselves up
like a salve for sore souls?
How can I go on pretending
now that these eyes
have beheld what might be
if only I dare to reach?
Voices of the crowd
drown out the calling
only by means of suffocation.

What breath am I allowing
to be withheld from me
when I would offer it up
willingly to the sights
that stun into the kind of silence
that is sacred in its own right?

IN THE NAME OF FEAR

I come back to this place
time after time
drawn in like the fool
I should know better than to be again.
Even the farthest corners of the earth
can't seem to lend me the escape I crave.
I wish to be locked away this day
and for the rest of them to come.
Time has proven to me
that I may never be someone
accustomed to what this world demands.
Lost in these green fields
where cell service cannot leech into me,
I get the barest taste of what free could be.

Erica Adelaide Johnson

I am propelled to fearlessness
in the name of fear itself
for I have never been more fearful
than standing in the presence of
all that I may have gotten so wrong.
There is only the one chance you see,
but that has never offered comfort to me.
I am a captive of all my errors
in the name of careful consideration.
My own best intentions have left me
little more than a shell of who I in my youth,
dreamed so fervently to be.

POTIONS AND POISON

I am emotion.

Could this all be some potion?

I am angry for the stories not mine to tell.

I am sorrowful for the satires drowned out.

I am anguished by the ages

stripped from me by my own cruel thoughts.

So, I take another sip

of the poison that fuels these lies

but dulls the way they cut into my mind.

Even my reflection stands hushed

as my knuckles turn white

gripped tight to the edge of the vanity

and my own sanity as it sinks into the drain

reminding me of all the burdens

that are draining me.

THE STONE

What if my hardened heart
is not what it seems?
Though I am alone,
I have never been able to be the stone.
I am the first leaves of spring wet with dew
overcome by the late season frost
that seeks to claim me.
Survive I have, but I wonder yet
if that has been my poison
drank down in the days after
the battle was done.
In the quiet, I am still fighting,
but the war has waged so, so long.
I grow weary for the rest
I no longer know how to have.

CEASE TO KNOW

The glow of you creeps in
soft like the lantern's light.
It reminds me that the best things
have a way of making themselves
so well-known with ease
that you cease to know
what it was before they were so.
As the sun slips
softly into the horizon's embrace
so do I seek to still myself
in the silky silence
of sleep and silt alike.

POSSESS

I wrap the golden ribbon

tighter round my hand

until the blood drips from my fingertips.

I marvel at the staining

and wonder.

If I cannot possess the end result,

might I mark each toil in this way?

At least then I cannot be denied

the existence of the journey.

ENCROACH

Even as I am surrounded
by what once brought me
so much solace,
I am overcome
endlessly by the anxieties
as they encroach relentlessly.
Why is it that I cannot
find within myself the ability
to push them away
if only for a moment of peace?

Erica Adelaide Johnson

I have found only new sources
of worry that wear away at me
as if my desperate need
to escape them only lures
new ones to me.
It seems I must remove myself
from the places that seek
to spread themselves
well past their appointed portion
of my precious time.
Might such a thing truly be mine
to take hold of once more
and if so, will my grip prove firm?

PARALYZED

I once considered the realization
of my dreams to be nonexclusive.
If anything, I knew my passions
to be destined to align.
For what other reason
would they be planted
so purposefully in me?
The weight of these years
has since shaken my resolve.
Could it be that I must forfeit the many
if any may stand a chance of success?
It is in this way that I find myself
paralyzed by indecision.

Erica Adelaide Johnson

How am I to choose
which parts of myself to abandon?
Which fragments of my heart
do not deserve their chance to live?
Try as I may to seize the hope
graciously poured out to me,
day by day, I find its scarcity growing.

NOVELTY

With the flood of visitors
that came in the following weeks,
I feared the person I had fought
all those lonely years to protect
would be swept away with them.
What if they came and saw
and took all the special pieces with them?
Worse yet, what if their clandestine nature
was all the worth that they held?
Could I bear to see the precious parts
of the heart I held reduced to nothing
more than a short-lived novelty?

Erica Adelaide Johnson

BLINDED

Tears brim in eyes
that have allowed themselves
to be blinded.
Eyelids close to shy away
from what glared at them,
like turning from something
ever made it less real.
Squint now you guileless girl
who strains to see
what has always been before you.
Why do you struggle so
for something that should have been
yours all along?

Romanticized Ruin

How can a thing promised
be something that eludes you so?
It has been here all along
just past arm's reach.
The soul must stretch
to capture what belongs to it.

Erica Adelaide Johnson

OUTCAST

I know I should lay this burden down,
let it lie still in the ground
with the past pressures that proved poison,
but what if it grows foreign to me,
as so many of the things
I left have?

Could I really bare
to be the outcast
of my own suffering?
I don't mean to cling to it,
but it feels like the only thing
that has truly been mine
all along.

DYING IN THE NIGHT

Through the door
I rush to see just a glimpse
of another day
dying in the night.

I feel it fleeing from me
as I give chase to everything
that seems to be pulled from me.

I drive like mad
into the setting sun
wishing that another day
wasn't done.

Erica Adelaide Johnson

I know I shouldn't mourn it,

but I can't help but feel

that there should be more to it.

DIVINE DIRE DIRECTION

The sand is littered with broken shells
sharp enough to slice straight through
to the bitter truth
of how it was never necessary
to be this way
only foolishly interpreted
as some divine dire direction.

The world laughs at me
and all the things I have lost
by stealing them from myself,
a hundred smiles
and a few dozen laughs,
still yet, the many opportunities
I let slip through the cracks.

Erica Adelaide Johnson

I was naive to think my own
rudimentary patches
would ever seal the leak
of life seeping through
this riddled hull,
my skull the doomed vessel
slowly capsizing.

A DREAM REALIZED

What is left in the aftermath
of a dream realized?
My own cursed perception
steals the joy of the moments
long sought after
like a vindictive thief.
The experience turns bitter
in the briefest space between
existence and the sweet sip of liveliness.
It makes me doubt the breath
in my own lungs this given minute.
How far-fetched does it seem then
that I may already be embraced
deep within the soil
I so wished to pass beneath my feet?

Forgive me I beg.
For all the aspirations I toil
to bring to fruition,
a hundred more I have spoiled for myself
and for you as well.
Now, among the clouds,
my heart seems fit to pound itself to dust.
The air itself is thick with all the many
things I fear I have forgotten
and the judgment that awaits
when I return to the ground.
Heavier still is the knowledge
that a dream realized may
ever be lost to me.

For what I have seen and known
sours in the wake of what I must return to.
To know the fullness is to feel the void
vast beneath my feet.
How it overwhelms me
to know the emptiness
that looms before me
when the plenty was mere inches
from my outstretched hand just days before.

Erica Adelaide Johnson

I WAS NEAR

What if I told you I was near,
the reflection of shiny prismatic colors
bursting through this haze of gray?

Would you understand then
that I am more myself now,
than I have ever been,
    but also, more alone,
        more different,
            more unattainable as well?

This is the shocking degree,
the need of animosity
that leaves me circling
in proximity to a world alien to me.

I find myself wandering these empty streets
down desolate alleyways
mesmerized by the slow satire
straining against the ever
persistent pressure of time.

As if the seconds themselves
have a weight to them, I sense it.
The ages are upon us
as they always have been
and as they will continue to be.

Erica Adelaide Johnson

HALLOWED HALLS

The sad truth of it
is that I have haunted these
hallowed halls for years
as if they would finally
break themselves open
to speak to me of the secrets
that might mend
my broken pieces
if only I were made to understand.
But I have come to realize
    my hesitation, and perhaps
        my expectation
            was the killing thing
that bled my own ambition
to oblivion.

Somewhere in the hurt,
I began to doubt myself.
In every facet,
and in the rays of light
that illuminated dust
in those lonely spaces,
I allowed myself to be comforted
in knowing I had failed.
It is only now that I realize
true success is only born
from the rubble of failure.
For without our stumbling
we might never
come to define success
for ourselves.

Erica Adelaide Johnson

AVALANCHE

I can't seem to shake this notion
that every moment I spend
should have been spent differently,
and as those missed opportunities
continue to accumulate,
I know that the avalanche
that finally buries me is inevitable.
In the midst of this paranoia,
I have managed to isolate
as I struggle to grip my sanity
while this threat looms before me.
It has only recently occurred to me
that there will be no one searching for me,
no hand to pull me from the packed snow.

Romanticized Ruin

So, now I sleep with a shovel
because somehow, I've grown accustomed
to saving myself even as I
am the source of my own ruin.
Each morning I pick splinters
from my palm because clinging tight
has been the only thing I've ever
been strong enough to do.

PATCHWORK

I would tell you that it feels like I am dying,
but that seems a bit dramatic.
After all, aren't we all?
I can't say how every morning
I find another snag in the frail fabric
of the false persona I cling to.
Strange how when you find yourself
unraveling
you become obsessed with patchwork,
like finding the right material
will solve every problem that looms.

I should know better.
I've been stitching up holes
for as long as I can remember,
and they never hold for long.
I am beginning to wonder
if there is a limit
to the mending that can be done.

NECESSITY

There are days I must wonder
if this unsettling within me
will ever find a way to quiet itself,
or if I will feel
perched on the edge endlessly.
I don't want to believe that this uncertainty
is the destiny I am faced with.
But if it is mine to realize
then surely, I possess within me
the courage to thrive on this perilous point.

As the days turn to months
and the months turn to years,
it seems that one of the grandest toils
that this life presents each of us
is the unearthing of the potential
that so often lies hidden
until necessity drives it to the light.
If it feels impossible now,
as so many of the challenges we face do,
we must remember that there is an
abundance of capability to be harvested
from the very fabric of our making.
We cannot guess the bounty
each season may bring, but we can trust
that necessity will be provided for.

UNANSWERED

The shovel discarded in the garden calls to me.
Could I wrap these bloody, blistered palms
once more around the handle
that always splinters?
Might this be the season
that the weeding finally takes?
Could I dig deep enough this time
to bury all this darkness for good
and trust it tamed
by the scorching summer sun?
Could I survive one more winter
if this haunting hopelessness
managed to escape the frozen ground
yet again?

If I kept the fire burning
all those many dark nights,
would it be enough to keep it at bay?
Would it ever truly subside and die,
or is the very life of me
and that deep desire to destroy it
all the sustenance it will need
for however many years lie ahead?
I guess the only real question worth asking
is if I can summon the strength
to answer that call
even in the presence of all these questions
that can only go
unanswered.

TRANSLUCENCY

I never knew the vulnerability
that came with translucency
until there were parts of me
stretched so thin
there was no more hiding of them.
Now I am bare
to the forces beyond my control,
if ever there was anything that fell within it.
I think that too was perhaps a fantasy,
a fixation with the sole purpose
of providing distraction
from the paralyzing fear
that is navigating a life as your own
when it has always been
a matter of circumstance.

LEFT TO RUIN

Misconstrued monstrosities
fill the mirrors in my home.
Reflections have grown ravenous
in the remnants of rage
that tore through every page.
What could be left to say
when the echoes of what erupted
have long since faded into the white noise?
There is no living soul here
to hear these tragedies,
only the tired frames of forgotten foes.

Erica Adelaide Johnson

There are cobwebs inhabiting every corner
of mind and body and dwelling.
All that was once held dear
now left to ruin, but I'm sure
I will find ways to romanticize that as well.

Section IV:
Mausoleum of
Memories

Erica Adelaide Johnson

MUSEUM TURNED MAUSOLEUM

Nothing prepared me
for the hollowness
that would inhabit these halls,
how I would pace in the shadows
hidden behind the drawn curtains
daring glimpses at the life
beyond the walls of this
museum turned mausoleum.
Now the collection
I once treasured has
taken to tormenting me.
In seeking to preserve their memory,
I have granted life to them once more.

I believed their time come and gone,
but the strife has surfaced
in the shifting sun's rays
that break through each day
illuminating the dust of these
unsettled graves.
Instead of honoring them,
I have allowed myself to become
their hostage.

MY DOOMED DAYS

For years I have haunted these
hallowed halls erected
in my doomed days.
The echoes of footsteps sound
even now past the remnants
of the glass casings
that once held my priceless pains.
For when one is left with so little,
they learn to cling to what is left.
Pain and her faithful partner in shame
fed each other in the dim lit showrooms.

These very rooms remained locked away,
except for the few that managed
to wear away at the glass
with one too many well-placed taps
that led to cracks that spilled my miseries.
I have stood face to face
as the waters welled and overwhelmed.
I never realized that one can't really move on
when their past is so well preserved
to be revisited again and again
in the lonely dark corners of their collection.

Erica Adelaide Johnson

FADE

Call these dandelions dead weight
as my numb fingers smooth
the winter mud from your name.
We are all destined for the same.
Our most magical of moments
condensed to a grave left unvisited
until the tally shifts
from the land of the living
to the bones beneath the earth
packed little by little each day.
It was so easy to imagine
before death became a personal encounter,
that our mark would remain,
but it is clear now,
how even the very best of us begin to fade.

PIECES

I am still who I was
even if the reflection
is interrupted with more ripples
than it once was.
My surface is not stagnant,
and that is something worth rejoicing in.
Just because I do not recognize
this version of myself
does not mean that it is any less of me
or the true self intended for me.
Today I hope to heal
just a fraction from the person
who feels such shame for
letting down a version of themselves
that no longer exists.

In life they tell you

that some relationships will fade.

It is inevitable that you will

lose a few people along the way.

What they fail to say

is that you will lose pieces of yourself too,

and ultimately, that's okay.

You are also discovering

new pieces every day.

Some are destined to be more beautiful

than you ever imagined,

capable of filling a space in your composition

you didn't even realize was vacant.

FAMILIAR

I was so worried for so long
that if I finished telling this story
that it would truly be the end.
Really, I wasn't ready to face
the day that I no longer
felt the anger so raw
in the fabric of my making
or the ache that lingered
long after the wrongs were
well and done.
If I let them go,
what would lie ahead of me?
What could come next
if I stopped reliving what had passed?
But my story will carry on.

Erica Adelaide Johnson

There are entire chapters
that I have not considered
because all I could see for myself
was the damage that had been done.
My heart is changing even now,
and what used to scare me
is not nearly as fearsome
as the thought that I might
relinquish the possibility of growth
to cling to this misery
simply because it is familiar.

INTERPRETATIONS

Success is a very personal interpretation
of which a key element
is the painful lesson
in recognizing that this interpretation
faces far more criticism
that many of our other decisions.
People are so quick to speak
of celebrating our unique perspective,
but that so often fails to apply
to the grander picture of our lives.
Take your coffee how you like.
Speak your mind on the dividing topics.
Offer up your experiences to the masses
for sake of some elevated insight.

Erica Adelaide Johnson

It is a very raw thing
to chase your ideal life
when it falters from the path
we are told is right.
As hard as we wish it so,
there is no right path for all of us.
The steps we take alone
are sometimes the most influential
for ourselves and for our contribution
to that greater whole
we so desperately wish to be a part of.

SHELTERED SHAME

Hands do quiver in the moments before.
Action is inevitable, and
true feeling can no longer be ignored.
I break myself open like the geode
long buried deep within the earth
that has held my secrets,
that has sheltered my shame.
All of my fear bleeds into the open,
and I can no longer deny
that every one of these smiles
has been tacked perfectly into place
because I have had a lifetime of practice.
But the strain has grown,
and the time has come for this smile to falter
so that I might find its true shape.

WEIGHT

How do I express the weight I feel
at the beginning and end of each day?
Gone are the moments of weightlessness,
faded as they have in the dawning
of the life that I should embrace.
An explanation was never my obligation
but rather, my obstacle.
In the absence of my worries
revolving around the interpretations
others might offer up to me uninvited,
I was able to open myself up
to not just the fear of what was to come
but the excitement and possibility of it as well.

ENTANGLED

I emerge somber in the fading light
for there are promises
kissing possibility goodbye.
I always hoped the day would come
that I would find within myself
the ability to finally lay these burdens to rest.
It feels different than I imagined it might,
but perhaps that is just my own
lack of foresight.
Healing is a fickle and frustrating experience,
a hallowed mass of hollowness and happiness
entangled so that none knows
which is truly winning.
Somewhere along the curving path,
I became at ease with the switch backs.

Erica Adelaide Johnson

No real progress ever seemed to take shape
on the straight and narrow portions.
I suppose it is fitting,
that this last great leap was made
as the fire of September's sun landed dim
on yet even more unfamiliar terrain.
Make no mistake, the journey is not done.
In fact, I believe wholeheartedly
that it never will be.
But after such turmoil,
I feel I have reached the end of one road
as it gives way to another.
What lies ahead is a welcome new direction,
and I am ever grateful for the paths
that continue to unfold.

BUOYANT BELIEFS

The waters rise now
to remind me that I have always
been the kind that swims
even when the grace to keep going
abandons me to the surf.
Buoyant are these beliefs
of better days to come
though I know not where from.
In time my own mind might grant me
a perspective shifted to the light.

VIGIL

The empty courtyard stands still,
but she remembers the bustle of life
just as surely as I remember
the foolish swell of possibility
that spills in youth each moment.
In the present, she stands vigil
over the many lives
come and gone,
the lived and lost
that paced the cobblestones
still yet heavy on the soil.

Romanticized Ruin

Indentations can be felt on the structure itself,
for history is a living thing
growing deeper and older
with each breath a visitor dares to take
offered like some anonymous tribute
to the story that shall outlive us all.
A culmination of the aches
that fill the bones of the masses
lie like unuttered whispers
swaying in the breeze
and clinging desperately
to the branches above.

SEARCH

My knees hit the ground hard
as life seems to crush me
just a bit more.
I kneel in search of some shred of peace
in this endless monotony,
desperate to find some meaning
laced beneath the routine.
Might it provide proof
that all of this served some
higher purpose?
The more I allow myself to fall
the closer I feel to the stars.

I think perhaps they whisper to me
even as their shine is hidden,
faded out in the dark distance.
Could it be that what I was
searching for was perspective?
Now that I have freed myself
from the aches of ages passed,
might I find the peace
present in the smallest wonders
of each and every day?

Erica Adelaide Johnson

ASPIRATIONS

What are our aspirations
but some carefully crafted creature
that grows with each glance attracted
when our excitement glows a bit too bright
in just the right light?
They encourage you to follow your passions,
but the world shrinks
away from the passionate,
because this chasing of a passion
was never meant to be
fuel to your own flame.
We were meant to fashion our course
for the sake of achieving greater success
only in terms of what we could produce
for the whole.

We were conditioned to be cogs
in the machine.
Our passions were never
meant to be our own.
We were never meant to strive for goals
outside the scope of what was
expected of us,
but those are the only times I feel alive.
Now, we collectively are precariously close
to leaping from the edge of expectation,
for the riches promised to us
pale in comparison to the wealth
that lives in the simple act of living.

Erica Adelaide Johnson

FLESH AND BONE

Strange how the silence can strangle
sure as your own hand that claws
at the base of your neck
like you can somehow carve
these feelings from your skin.
They have taken on a life of their own
in the space between your flesh and bone.
I fear no separation may come
this side of the grave.
The loosening of such a grip
seems only possible in the passing
far away from the tightening
I have always felt.

Romanticized Ruin

Could something freer truly exist
out there in the beyond
where time has ceased
to have the upper hand?
Could all my misgivings
lose their weight there
where all that ever mattered
was what remained at the core
past all the crooked interpretations
of our fallacious intentions?

Erica Adelaide Johnson

GARDEN OF RUIN

The phone call was rehearsed
but never made.
The healing of wounds was theorized,
but never placed into practice.
Words were granted
to all these unspoken questions
but still, nothing happened.
It is the mystery that drives the misery
when the possibility plants itself
firmly in the garden of ruin.
Better will never bloom,
but the soil is true.
Perhaps a fruit of understanding
is all that was ever intended to take root.

RELIEF

Tears prick my eyes as you go.
I can't help but wonder
why relief feels so much like regret.
Cut from the same cloth I suppose.
Am I a hypocrite for the way the past
hangs onto me like shackles?
I do my best to grow stronger,
and it is easier to think I succeed
in your absence.
The proximity of you in this new manner
reminds me painfully of the loss I still feel
from the time when you were not
who you have become.

What I wonder most
is if you and I will ever find a way
to show our true selves to each other,
but even then, would we dare believe
our perception of such a thing?
We are shapeshifters of the worst kind,
born of desperation
to prove our own independence
and fuel our own idea
that we are somehow better suited.
When truly we are suited only for solitude.

MOURNING GARDEN

Statues stare as I pace
up and down the stairs
of the mourning garden.
No, I can't erase
the haste I feel
to get to this place.
See, home has lost all hold.
I am aimless and alone,
but I've never felt more free
in the bones that brace me.
I am the frozen lake
hardened in the heart of winter.
The thaw cannot threaten me here.

I have made my place among the
undesirable nooks and crannies.
I find myself graced in the presence
of the golden graves of who I was.
This is the death of me
but the only true life
I've ever known.

WORTHY

In the future
that I am just now
beginning to see as possibility,
what will the little loves
see in me?

Will I be the pillar of strength
I wish to be so desperately,
or will the broken remnants of me
never find their way back together?

Might my own shortcomings
be the influences that mold me
to be the person worthy
of offering a way past them?

Erica Adelaide Johnson

LAYERS

There are layers to you and I
just as there are layers to the lies.
The lessons you left me with
present themselves in a new light
each and every day
as I learn to live with the pain.
I no longer dwell on it,
but its ache is a part of my
innermost movements.
For so long I could not imagine
that its sting might dull.
Even more, I would not have dared
to find some comfort
in what such feeling gave way to.

But I cannot ignore
that there are blessings
in the way I have been shaped by it,
for I would not forfeit
the strength that was unearthed
once the ash was cleared.

DICTIONARY

My mind's dictionary is flawed.
I will spend the better part of my adulthood
ripping pages roughly from their resting place.
I stoke the fire now
and toss a few lies into the flame,
the false permanence of ink
fading in the smoke
that billows softly into the night air.
It is here, page by page,
that I purge what has haunted me.
It is here that I learn that harsh,
freeing truth of impermanence,
and in turn, revel
in the precious fleeting moments.

Soon, I will take up the pen again.

Gingerly I will craft the new definitions

that shall be stored inside

the deepest parts of my soul

that I hope to preserve.

In time, I might pass on this dictionary.

I only hope that the inheritance I leave

does not prove corrosive like so many do.

Erica Adelaide Johnson

RUINED RELICS

All that remains of my priceless museum
are the ruined relics left behind
and the memories buried in my mind.
I swore I wouldn't shed another tear,
but it's been another year
since the hurt first seared my soul.
I'm slowly learning to show some
consideration for myself,
because sometimes the best we can do
is mourning in the moonlight.
But I know another day shall dawn.
And one day, I will visit these ruins
without feeling the need to collect
pieces to take with me.

Romanticized Ruin

This space in my history
will always hold some part of me,
but it will no longer determine my path.
There is far too much
possibility for new construction
for me to waste one more moment
trying to rebuild this failed structure.
There is beauty in recognizing
when treasure has had its time to shine
and that the tarnish will only serve
to secure its ability to resonate
its ever transforming message
in the days to come.

Erica Adelaide Johnson

SHRINE

I approach like a mourner
to the sacred shrine.
My past cannot be found
gilded in gold but
looms like a palace preserved
in cold alabaster stone
aimed to remind me of a thousand
small deaths endured
to breathe just this one
precious breath even as it
escapes ragged from these lungs.

See, I am thankful for the gasping
for it serves as proof of all the life
that I still have to lose.

Romanticized Ruin

For all the things drained from me
so much still courses through these veins,
and for all the tortured dreams
dead and buried
there are a thousand more
waiting to take their place.

I used to think I was cursed
with the burden of conflicting passions,
but I now see the beauty in knowing
I will never truly run out
    of things to find worthy
        of striving,
           of suffering,
               of sacrificing for.

RESOLVE

I have created beautiful things before,
and I will create them again.
There is no rushing this resolve,
and this lesson in quiet resistance
to my own doubt is shaping
the next chapters of my story
in ways I cannot see in the thick of it.
The progress will at times be slow,
but that does not mean there is not
a purpose to the steady pace
set by the innermost workings of your being.
Listen to yourself in the silence
past the noise of the anxious thoughts.

Despite their volume,
they have never truly been able
to drown out your purpose.
You should take the things
that you have accomplished
as evidence of what you are capable of
and of the wonders yet to come,
rather than let them discourage you.
I tell you dear, your time is not done.
The person you are today
is just beginning.
Who you were all those years ago
has had their time.

Don't let comparison to a past self derail you.
This is your reminder
to be kind to yourself
in these stages when you are welcoming
the stranger that lives in your bones.
They have a right to be there
just as much as those that
no longer inhabit them did.
Don't allow yourself to be blind to their worth
simply because you refuse to move past
the grief of what once was.

HALLOWED GROUNDS

I wander in the night, guided only by torchlight
and find myself among the tombstones
that rise above this resting place
as stark silhouettes standing vigil.
My hand brings the flame close
to read the inscription carved in stone.
These are hallowed grounds
despite the horrific events that crafted them.
The state of reverie that descends now
is not marked by romanticism
but a reminiscence that recognizes a deeper
purpose beyond the ruins that remain.
This site is a memorial
to the strength that brought me here
when it seemed an ill-fated hope to hold.

Erica Adelaide Johnson

CURATOR

I had considered myself lost
to the tomb of my own traumas,
but the beauty in the transformation
of the museum that once stood
as a monument
was the gift of a resting place
for all the pain I had buried myself with.
It took time to break through,
but on the outside of these walls,
I feel that I no longer have to mourn.
Rather, this feels like the right way
to honor the events that shaped me.
I will never forget them.
I don't want to.

I have forgotten far too many things
for the sake of my own survival,
but I don't have to sit in solitude
with them any longer.
I can revisit their lessons
without subjecting myself to their horrors.
This is the beginning
of a brand-new collection.
I will always find myself
a curator of memories,
but I know now that the value of a collection
lies only in the impact it serves to share.
Without new pieces our growth is stagnant.

We can never serve as the judge
of which of our creations
will be elevated to masterpieces.
We are charged to honor the creations
each as they are, for the imperfections
serve as inspiration,
and the cycle carries on and on
in each and every soul
seeking to make sense of the sight
for themselves.

Join the journey at
ericaadelaidejohnson.com.

www.ingramcontent.com/pod-product-compliance
Lightning Source LLC
LaVergne TN
LVHW041215080426
835508LV00011B/966